# ALPIN]
# IN
# SINKS AND TROUGHS

## JOE ELLIOTT

Line drawings by Duncan B. Lowe

Editor

Christopher Grey-Wilson

The Alpine Garden Society

To my Father
Whose enthusiasm started my
interest in plants
And to my Wife
Whose tolerance and encouragement
keep it young

# In the beginning . . .

Though my father, Clarence Elliott, would not, I am sure, have claimed to have initiated the idea of growing alpines in stone sinks and troughs, there can be little doubt that he did more than any other single person to popularise and expand this now universal activity.

One of the earliest and possibly one of the largest collections of alpines grown in these old vessels was owned by the 'Mistress Mary Saunders' mentioned by Reginald Farrer in *My Rock Garden* as the finder of a fine white form of *Primula farinosa*. She was a keen alpine plantswoman and seems usually to have devoted each trough or quern (for some of them were quite small) to a single species, giving most of them a diet of equal parts of leaf-mould and gravel. My father paid several visits to her garden and, though I do not remember him saying so, I think it was probably Mrs. Saunders' collection of plants and the way she grew them that sowed the germ of the idea he was to exploit and expand so successfully. I remember that in the early and mid 1920s he went many times to Yorkshire to hunt out these treasures in farmyards and elsewhere and would send a lorry from Stevenage, where we then lived, to bring them back.

It was at about this time, too, that the humble old stone kitchen sinks started being removed from houses to be replaced by the more hygienic glazed ones. These proved a boon when the supply of pig and cattle troughs began to run low. They were always cut from real stone, which was congenial to plant life, and though on the shallow side with an inside depth of little more than three inches as a rule, they were of convenient size and were plentiful. In almost any builder's yard of those days one could find several and, until the craze gathered speed, they could often be had for the asking, to save the builder the bother of breaking them up or dumping them.

For as long as I can remember our house at Stevenage was always surrounded by sinks and troughs of all shapes and sizes, perched on any convenient low wall, lining the path edges or making a feature of a difficult garden corner. Many of the smaller ones, perhaps only eight or ten inches across, would have only a single plant in them; but the larger ones (and we had some real monsters) had a wide variety of plants growing in them, with rocks carefully selected and arranged to form the miniature trough gardens we are so familiar with today.

It was some time in the late 1920s, too, that my father was involved in another short-lived venture which must have helped to convince him of the enchantment held by a mixed collection of jewel-like flowering alpines arranged in a small space. Reggie Wells, the well-known potter whose Soon pottery is now much sought after by collectors, was a friend of my father's. He was greatly influenced by the Chinese potter's art and, as well as fascinating animals and pots in the Chinese tradition, was making a number of shallow bowls like the ones Japanese bonsai trees are grown in today. As so often happens, a number of these were damaged in the firing process and Wells found himself with a lot of these beautiful objects which were unsaleable. They varied in size from ten up to as much as 50cm. in length or width, and were anything from 5—15cm. deep. Father suggested that he should plant them up as miniature rock gardens, an idea that the ever-enterprising Wells jumped at. At that time Wells had a shop in Bond Street to sell his wares and I remember father setting off for London with boxes and boxes of pot-grown alpines in bud and flower, together with all the necessary paraphernalia of soil, rocks, stone chippings — everything in fact except his kitchen sinks. With these, in the stock-room behind the shop, he created beautiful effects in the damaged bowls and they were sold for high prices — up to twelve or fifteen guineas, which in those far-off days was quite big money. I suspect that most of them were bought by Londoners and kept in their flats, so they probably did not have a very long life; but whilst they lasted they must have been bewitching novelties.

# Real Gardening

As the popularity of this new method of growing alpines increased, more and more sinks and troughs appeared at Six Hills Nursery and my father wrote many articles on them in the gardening press. We soon found that, quite apart from the intrinsic charm, even to a relative non-gardener, of having a rock garden in miniature, growing alpines in troughs was a method that was often successful with difficult and tricky plants where other methods failed. Special soil mixtures could be made for individual plants and more easily contained in the confines of a trough than in the open rock garden. Perhaps there is some psychological factor involved too; the plants are more isolated and nearer eye-level, where they can be seen and inspected; special treatments can be given more easily than in the wider spaces of the garden. I certainly remember many plants that are considered capricious growing with great vigour in the Six Hills troughs — *Campanula zoysii*, for instance, and *Viola delphinantha*: *Primula allionii* and *Campanula piperi* and, of course, many others. So trough gardening was becoming something not only to satisfy the whims of those who liked the look of these pretty objects, but a very real and valid means of growing difficult plants for the keen and knowledgeable plantsman.

# Chelsea Show

In the early 1930s my father started exhibiting trough gardens at Chelsea Flower Show. Each year, at this great Show, Six Hills Nursery put up a large rock garden on the rock garden bank and a smaller table rock garden in the marquee. Now we took a third space on the grass triangle opposite the rock gardens to display the stone troughs. By now the supply of easily available and cheap stone troughs and sinks was beginning to dry up, so father found a quarry where they could be cut to order. The stone was a soft, mellow limestone which weathered quickly and, though of regular shape, they were sufficiently rugged and tool-marked to avoid looking artificial. They were cut in three sizes, the smallest being about 45cm. by 30cm. and the largest some 90cm. long by about 45cm. wide. This regularity of size had the advantage that, after an individual trough had been sold at the Show, any particular arrangement of plants and rock could be approximately repeated for any subsequent customer who took a fancy to it. I remember with great pleasure the many days I spent before Chelsea making up these troughs, varying the plants and rock formation as much as possible to give a wide variety of shape and form. The majority of plants would be in flower or bud, of course, to give maximum impact for the Show, but I was always careful to include a few later and earlier flowerers so that buyers would get more prolonged enjoyment.

After a few years, however, the Royal Horticultural Society decided in their wisdom, or lack of it, that trough gardening was not real gardening and the place for these 'objects' was in the Sundries Avenue. My father's reaction was classic, explosive and unprintable. Trough gardens did not appear again at Chelsea under the Six Hills banner.

## Slab Gardens

There have been various adaptions of the main principles of trough gardening, perhaps the most significant of which was evolved by that great cricketer and gardener, the late Capt. Simpson-Hayward. He called it Slab Gardening. Instead of a stone trough he used a rectangular paving stone raised on stone pillars eighteen inches or so high. Around the perimeter of the paving stone he arranged small irregular pieces of rock, held in place by a small dab of concealed cement. These rocks held the soil on the slab and prevented its being washed off by heavy rain or the watering can. In the centre he could then arrange larger rocks in picturesque form to give pockets and crevices in which the plants could grow. In such a structure good drainage, the need for which is perhaps the one characteristic which all true alpines have in common, was automatic. These Slab Gardens could be of any size from 30cm. square to monsters 180cm. or more in length, though I doubt if a single slab could be found of that size. The really large ones are best made up of several paving stones of more modest size, suitably supported underneath and with half-inch gaps left between the inner edges for extra good drainage. Whether these ideas came to Capt. Simpson-Hayward spontaneously or were born of necessity through the scarcity of genuine old stone troughs, I am not sure. But certainly Slab Gardens are one answer to the present great difficulty — and expense — of acquiring the genuine article. They can be made to look charming and natural and many plants enjoy life in them.

## Glazed Sinks

A more recent innovation is to make use of the white, glazed kitchen sinks — suitably disguised, of course! It is a curious fact that, when sink gardening began, it was the old stone sinks which

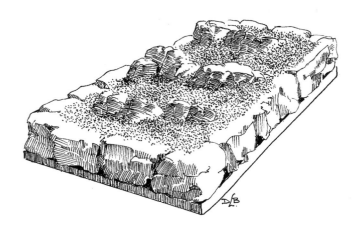

had become redundant and were available for gardening purposes. Nowadays the white glazed sinks which replaced them are themselves being replaced in most homes by the more modern stainless steel sink unit. One wonders what will be the next step in the evolution of the kitchen sink and what use we gardeners will make of the stainless steel units when they in turn become redundant. What on earth shall we do with the draining board end?

The means by which the glossy white hideousness of the glazed sinks can be disguised is by the use of what has come to be known as Hypertufa, which is a mixture of cement, sand and sphagnum peat. Experts in these matters tend to throw up their hands in horror at the thought of mixing cement with peat; they say the acidity of the peat and the alkalinity of the cement are incompatible and will react on each other. In spite of this, those who have used this mixture have found it quite excellent for the purpose. It can be made to look very like natural stone and after a year or two's weathering is difficult to distinguish from the real thing. From a gardening point of view it seems that the presence of the peat in some way counters the dislike that plant life in general has for raw cement.

Before starting operations the glazed sink must be scrubbed and thoroughly cleansed of any grease or other dirt that might remain from its original use. When quite dry it should be coated with a thin film of one of the modern bonding adhesives; Polybond or Unibond are equally good and can be bought from most ironmongers. Both are easily applied with a paint brush. It is essential to use the adhesive as it is almost impossible to make the Hyper-tufa stick directly to the smooth glazed surface. The Hypertufa it-self is made up as follows:

Two parts (by bulk) of moistened, sifted sphagnum peat.
One part coarse sand, or very fine grit.
One part of cement.

The ingredients should be thoroughly mixed whilst dry and then water added whilst further mixing goes on, until it is of such a consistency that it can be applied to the sides of the trough without

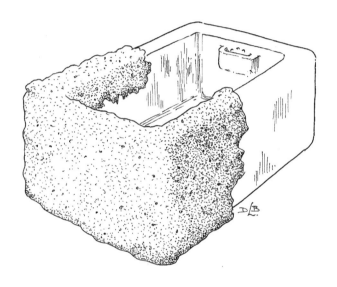

slithering off. It is not necessary to coat the whole inside of the troughs but the Hypertufa should be taken over the top and down the inside edge for a few inches so that when soil is eventually put into the sink (or shall we now call it a trough?) no white glazing will be visible. It is best to let the bonding material become dry or at least tacky before work starts and I find that half an inch of Hypertufa is ample thickness for both strength and durability. As the material begins to harden it can be worked with the fingers or a piece of wood or other tools into as realistic an imitation of a stone surface as you feel inclined.

Old troughs arranged on paving

Photos: Joe Elliott

Section of a well planted stone trough

Stone troughs planted with dwarf conifers and alpines          Photos: AGS Library

A stone trough planted with a collection of sempervivums

# Casting in Hypertufa

There is a further use for Hypertufa, however, and that is the casting of whole troughs in the material. I do not feel this is the place to go into details of this slightly more complicated process; anyway, it is one of the many things I have meant to do for a long time and never got round to doing. But there is an excellent article on the subject by S.E. Lilley in A Handbook of Rock Gardening published by the A.G.S. If you have not already got this publication you should hasten to acquire it (it was incorporated in the AGS *Bulletin*, 32:32-37, 1964. *Ed.*). It is full of interesting and useful information for all alpine enthusiasts. Mr. Lilley has a number of these pure Hypertufa troughs in his garden and when I visited him recently I found it almost impossible to tell which were the genuine stone ones and which were of his own making. If they are carefully and sensibly made in the first place, a year or two of weathering puts on such a good patina of moss and lichen that they become indistinguishable from the real thing. The very fact that they weather so well on the visible outside is an indication of just how much more congenial Hypertufa is to plant life than is a normal cement mixture. A trough cast in normal cement takes many years to lose its hard, grey, naked look and plant roots never like coming into contact with it. The addition of peat seems to make all the difference, both aesthetically and practically.

# Siting

Having acquired your trough, whether genuine stone or simulated, its siting is of prime importance. Unless you intend to grow only shade loving plants, and there are not many of these suitable for troughs, it should be in an open sunny position where it will not be in the shadows cast by trees or buildings for more than an hour or so each day. Above all, avoid overhanging trees or bushes; almost without exception alpines dislike drip from overhanging branches. A paved or gravel terrace is often an appropriate place, or troughs can make a suitable termination to a low stone wall, but they often look best on the edge of a lawn. This however presents difficulties with mowing and may entail laying a platform of paving stones flush with the grass. Apart from the nuisance of having to steer round the obstacle, no mower is made that can cut right up to the vertical sides of a trough or its supporting pillar, although modern strimmers perform the job reasonably well. An alternative, if the trough is to be on the edge of a lawn beside a path, is to cut out a semi-circle of grass and incorporate this into the path so that your trough is standing on gravel and paving, with a half-circle of mowable grass a foot or more from its sides.

## Support

Your trough will always look better if it is raised off the ground. It is quite a simple matter to build pillars of brick or stone; one pillar for a small trough but two or even three if it is a large or heavy one. The height of the pillars will depend on the depth of the trough itself. The aim should be to bring the top rim not less than 45 cm. or more than 55 cm. from the surrounding ground. If much higher than this it tends to look perched up and inelegantly balanced; if lower it loses importance and seems to be in a permanent squat. Even if you are lucky enough to acquire one of the large stone drinking troughs that used to stand about farmyards and which may be 45 or 50 cm. deep, it will look better raised off the ground if only by the thickness of a brick. This will also ensure that surplus water can drain out of the drainage hole, which it is essential to have in all troughs of whatever shape or size. Without this the soil will very quickly be converted into a nasty sour bog in which no

plant can possibly be happy. It is not a difficult process to make a hole; it is surprising how quickly one can chip away the stone with a cold chisel and a good heavy hammer. An electric drill fitted with a mason's drill can be a great help too. Make the hole at least 2.5cm. (1in.) wide if you can. Care must be taken when placing the trough on its supporting pillars that the holes do not coincide with the pillars and so have their purpose defeated. Be very careful, too, to see that the trough is bedded absolutely firmly on its support without any possibility of its being pushed over accidentally. Even a small trough, together with its soil and rocks, is a hideously heavy object to find on one's foot or leg and they are often things round which the children like to play. Occasionally I found visitors to my nursery using my troughs as squatting places. No doubt they imagined they were utilising only the outside rim of stone and were unaware how far their silly rumps protruded to the detriment of my plants. At such times I wished I had not made the troughs quite so secure on their supports and that they would gently slide off with their load.

## Soil and Drainage

So now your trough is firmly set in its open, sunny position, its drainage hole is free and the real fun begins! The first thing to do is to place a few large pieces of broken pot over the drainage hole, just as one would in a large flower pot, to obstruct the movement of soil and to allow the free passage of surplus water. Then cover the whole of the bottom with some coarse drainage material; broken pots if you have them or, failing this, coarse, washed gravel. The depth of this drainage layer will depend on the depth of your trough. If you are making up an old stone kitchen sink with an inside depth of only 5—7.5cm., you cannot afford to put more than a scattering of drainage material; if on the other hand you are dealing with something larger, having an inside depth of 20, 25 or more centimetres, you can, if you want, sacrifice up to a third of this depth to drainage, though 5—7cm. is usually sufficient. Next, place a couple of cm. or so of coarse peat siftings or an upside down turf over the whole lot. This is simply to ensure that the finer soil, which will go in next, does not filter down too easily into the drainage layer. The composition of the main body of the soil will rather depend on what you want to grow. If you just want a nice collection of fairly easy, bright alpines to give you a bright show for as long as possible, the John Innes potting compost is perfectly suitable and usually easy to obtain. If on the other hand you want to go in for some of the choicer, more exacting plants, some extra drainage may be needed. This can be added in the form of stone chippings or sharp grit. Personally I prefer chippings made from soft, porous rock. These not only assist the passage of free water through the soil but they retain an appreciable amount of moisture within themselves which the ever-questing roots of the alpines can draw on when the need arises: 6—9mm. chippings are

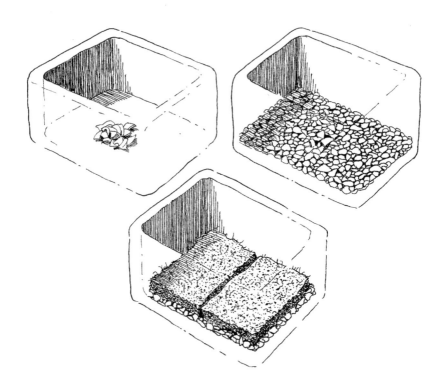

suitable and can be added to make up as much as a third of the total bulk of the soil. Provided you do not intend to grow any ericaceous or other lime-hating plants, limestone chips are probably best. They are generally more porous that granite or other non-limy chips and the great majority of plants grow more happily in a limy soil. But if lime-hating plants are to be grown the chippings must of course be granite or sandstone and the soil mixture itself must be lime-free.

If you prefer to make up your own soils, the basic mixture could be three parts by bulk of loam (preferably stacked and well-rotted turf) put through a 9mm. (3/8in.) sieve, two parts of moistened sphagnum peat and one of coarse sand or very sharp grit. This can be taken as a fairly basic mix for growing almost any alpine, either in a trough or elsewhere; additional refinements such as stone chips, extra sand, more peat and so on can then be added to suit the plants for which it is intended. It is vitally important when you are filling your trough with whatever soil mix you have decided on, that it should be really well firmed before any rock building or planting is started. If this is not done you will find that after a year or so the soil consolidates and sinks down, taking plants and rocks with it, so that they look sunken and forlorn with a several cms. wall of trough-side stone all round them. Firming is really a very simple task. Put in 5—7cm. of soil over the whole area and press down firmly several times with all the weight of your body on your two clenched fists, paying particular attention to the corners and sides (watch out for grazed knuckles, though!). Then spread another 5—7.5 cm. of soil, firm down again and repeat the process until the top is reached.

# Rock

The next important job is the selection of rock, for no trough can really look anything without a few carefully-chosen and well-placed rocks. Their purpose is practical as well as aesthetic, for many alpine plants like nothing better than to feel their roots exploring their way along the moist hidden surfaces on the cool undersides of rocks and stones. Without doubt the best rock for the purpose, if it can be found, is tufa, but it is, unfortunately, in very short supply and often hard to come by. It is a very quick-forming limestone formation which is found only in a few isolated parts of the country, including Derbyshire and North Wales. It has the two great advantages of being very soft and extremely porous. When newly quarried, any pointed instrument — even an old kitchen knife — will give sufficient purchase to bore small holes into it, and in these holes many naturally saxatile plants will grow better than by any other method that has so far been devised. In time the outer surface gradually hardens, but the inner core remains soft and porous so that plants growing in these holes can extend their roots right through the whole body of the rock, seeking and finding the moisture they are forever questing. It is probably the nearest garden equivalent we can offer to those plants that normally inhabit the chinks and crevices of a mountain cliff. A seedling of such a plant finding itself germinating in the wild on a tiny cranny of a cliff-face will quickly search with its roots for any minute fissure in the rock. It may be only a millimetre wide, but that is sufficient; in a relatively short time it will have produced an immense amount of root, possibly covering several square metres inside the rock face, with perhaps only a 15 cm. hummock of close-packed leaves showing on the surface. I am thinking particularly of such plants as the Aretian androsaces, *Physoplexis comosa*, *Potentilla nitida* and the like. Tufa offers a very fair imitation of these conditions so far as the root-run goes (the climatic conditions on the outer surface of the rock are another matter of course), the only difference being that on a natural cliff the roots will be spread out in a vast fan only a few millimetres thick, whereas in the tufa the roots can wander at will in all directions.

Unfortunately, like so many good things in life, tufa also has its disadvantages, perhaps the most maddening of which is the fact that it is not always entirely stable; you may find that odd pieces are crumbled by frost. This can be a great nuisance, particularly as it sometimes happens quite unpredictably after several years of weathering, when plants may be well established in it. This habit is also pretty galling, to say the least, when it occurs in one stone forming part of a group, for to replace it may mean pulling the whole group to pieces and disturbing established plants. Also tufa is a rock that must be placed in full sunlight; with even a small amount of shade, the constant inner moisture of the rock tends to encourage the growth of moss. In full sun, this is usually manageable and in fact gives a nice weathered appearance; in a small amount of shade it can get out of hand and smother choice plants.

If tufa is not obtainable one has to make do with whatever rock is available. Obviously if you live in a stone district the local rock is not only the most appropriate but also the most easily obtained and the cheapest. Try to choose good rugged shapes and do not be afraid of having at least one quite large rock in each trough. A few small rocks can never give the same effect as one really substantial piece surrounded by a few of lesser size. As a rough guide, in a trough say 90cm. by 60cm., you should have one key rock which is at least as large as two footballs, to make an easily understood analogy, and might weigh 15—20 kilos. Your aim should be to place your largest rock off centre and then arrange the smaller ones around and near it, leaving crevices about an inch wide between them, to furnish natural homes for many of your plants. When the plants are established in these crevices the illusion should be that you are looking at one large rock split up over the years by frost and weathering, on which plants have managed to find a foothold on the now nearly invisible crevices. Every rock should be well bedded into the soil, with its base fully covered, and firmed all round the edges with a trowel-handle or similar tool, before planting is started. In a large trough you can often get the best effect by forming two separate outcrops of different sizes, with a valley between; whilst in one of more modest size it may be better to have one important outcrop towards one end and then, in the flatter area left at the opposite end, to place one well-shaped, rugged rock in isolation. The variations are enormous and it can be the greatest fun moving the rocks around, fitting them in like a jigsaw puzzle till the ideal formation is found. My father summed it up well when he wrote 'The rock outcrops should sit down upon the soil like a contented cat'.

## Planting

Now comes the most important and interesting part of all; choosing your plants and putting them in position. The choice is enormous. What are the limits? Where to begin? Where to end? My own feeling is that the plants should be restricted to those which are small and slow-growing. There are plenty of other places in the garden for the strong vigorous growers and to me a trough garden is essentially a place where the small, tight-growing alpines can find a home where they will not be smothered by rampageous neighbours. As far as possible the whole scale should be kept down. This does not mean, of course, that the plants you grow in your troughs will in any way be lacking in a wide variety of form, shape or colour. They fall fairly easily into certain categories such as those which will trail down over the edges, others that will grow in the crevices; some will form carpets in the flatter areas and a few, but only a few, will be upright growing. These last are perhaps the most difficult to select and place. If overdone they can spoil the whole effect of the miniature garden but if rightly chosen and placed they can add a vital dimension to the whole effect.

## Bulbs

On the whole I think it is best to exclude bulbs from trough gardens. Though some of the tiny crocuses and narcissi can give a welcome splash of colour very early in the year, and if rightly placed may be in scale whilst in flower, their leaves are so often an unsightly, straggling mass. They can even become a danger if allowed to flop in a wet, soggy mass over choice moisture-hating neighbours. It is not a point I would be dogmatic about; it must be a matter of personal choice and convenience. What I am absolutely against, however, is the inclusion of any annuals. No matter how dwarf, bright or jewel-like they may be, no matter how convenient to fill in a blank space, they always look completely alien and out of place amongst real alpine plants.

## Conifers

Perhaps the most difficult of all plants to choose are the dwarf conifers. There is no doubt that the right dwarf, evergreen conifer, planted in exactly the right position, adds enormously to the effect of your miniature landscape. But choose the wrong one and you will very soon be in trouble. What it really boils down to is what is a dwarf conifer? And how dwarf is dwarf? It seems a pity, now that these engaging plants are becoming so popular, that a more exact system of classification could not be devised to give the un-initiated clearer guidance about the ultimate height and spread to which they will grow under normal conditions. There are now several reliable nurserymen who specialise in these plants and if you are in doubt the best thing is to seek one's advice about those which will remain of modest size for a reasonable amount of years. His first choice for a trough will almost certainly be *Juniperus communis* 'Compressa' and he will, of course, be absolutely right. Without question this is the most nearly perfect dwarf conifer for trough gardens, forming a beautifully upright little pointed column of blue-grey leaves; it will take many years to outgrow its allotted space. If you plant a 10—12 cm. specimen in new soil in a trough, it may increase its height by 2.5cm. or more for a year or two but, as the nourishment in the soil is gradually depleted, the rate of growth will slow down to little more than a centimetre a year. Even after ten or fifteen years it will seldom be more than about 30 cm. high. This rapid initial growth, followed by a gradual slowing down, will usually take place with whatever dwarf or miniature conifer you plant in a trough. All the same, one does not want to start off with a variety which, even with its roots restricted, will grow 90cm. in three years.

As a general rule there is not much that can be done about pruning back dwarf conifers when they have outgrown their space. Most of them resent such treatment and anyway their essential and individual form would be spoiled. About the only exception to this

is the prostrate junipers. Some years ago a friend gave me w
said was a very dwarf, compact, slow-growing form of our ..
*Juniperus communis,* a cutting of which he had collected on Llewed
in the Welsh mountains. I planted it on the edge of one of my very
large troughs and it stayed quite compact making little growth for
the first few years. Then it suddenly got into gear, put its accelera-
tor down and roared off in all directions. The branches growing
over and into the trough were removed and those tumbling over
the edge were allowed to remain. Now, some twentyfive years later,
it is a fascinating old veteran, cascading down nearly to the path
45cm. below and cloaking two-thirds of the trough-side with its
evergreen blanket of blue-grey needles. It in no way resents the removal of branches with which it may try to embrace plants in the
body of the trough, nor does this treatment spoil its character; it
rather adds to it. Semi-natural bonsai, perhaps?

The same treatment could no doubt be given to *Juniperus
communis* 'Depressa Aurea', though I have not tried it myself. It is
a stronger grower than my Llewed 'dwarf' and would thus need
even more severe pruning. But it is a most beautiful plant with
brilliant golden spring growth, which holds its colour well into the
summer before turning bronze for the winter. One would need a
big trough, though!

One fact that must be faced; whichever dwarf conifer you
choose it will probably cost you more than any other single plant
you are likely to put in your trough. Even the relatively cheap ones
will cost two or three times as much as most other alpines, which
is logical when you come to think of it. They are likely to have
taken at least two or three times as long for the nurseryman to
have brought to saleable size. Added to which, by some curious
plant logic, the slower a conifer grows the more difficult it is to
root and the less cutting material it produces. Take *Juniperus communis* 'Echiniformis' for instance; it is one of the slowest-growing
of all conifers and quite the most difficult to root, even with the
most modern aids to propagation. If you should ever be offered a
plant of this, snap it up, regardless of cost, and watch it with bated
breath for the next twenty years whilst it builds itself up into a
spiny dome the size of a tennis ball. Exhale only when it has put
on sufficient growth for you to remove a cutting.

*Abies balsamea* 'Hudsonia', or slightly differing forms under
such names as *A.b.* 'Nana' or *A.b.* 'Prostrata', are all very slow-
growing, either bun-shaped or semi-prostrate, with glossy deep-green
foliage arranged with beautiful symmetry. If the true plant can be
found, *Chamaecyparis obtusa* 'Ericoides' is another suitable candi-

date with pretty, spiky, light green foliage of both juvenile and adult form; but the nomenclature of this group is as chaotic and unstable as anywhere in the dwarf conifer world. *Chamaecyparis obtusa* 'Nana Gracilis' is to me the most beautiful of all slow-growing conifers, with lustrous green fans of foliage forming themselves into picturesque shapes, but it will soon outgrow all but the largest troughs. This is not the case with *Chamaecyparis obtusa* 'Intermedia' which forms a dense round bushlet of rich deep green. I have had a plant of this in my alpine house for more than thirty years and it is still no more than 30cm. across. This extreme lack of size is no doubt due to food shortage as much as anything, for though it is watered regularly it seldom gets more nourishment than an occasional pinch of Hoof and Horn. It has not been potted-on or had its soil changed for nearly ten years now. The surprising thing is that in spite of this sadistic treatment it repays me by looking completely healthy and most attractive.

Chamaecyparis pisifera 'Nana' (or should it be 'Compacta'?) is another really slow grower, flat-topped and bun-shaped with pleasant medium-green leaves with an almost feathery look. A specimen of this has been growing in the corner of one of my larger troughs for seventeen or eighteen years and is still only about 30 cm. across and about 15 cm. high. It looks happy and healthy in spite of little encouragement other than regular watering.

Only one *Cryptomeria* is worth considering, *C. japonica* 'Vilmoriniana'. Though H.J. Welch in *Dwarf Conifers* quotes it as reaching 1 m. in height, it is unlikely to attain anything like that within the confines of a trough. It makes a dense, rounded bushlet of short, firm leaves, closely packed and of a fairly bright, glossy green, and often tends to take on bronze-purple shades during the winter.

Most dwarf *Picea* species will outgrow the proportions of a trough. *Picea glauca* 'Albertiana Conica' is a well-known and well-loved charmer, forming a dense pyramid whose new spring growth is vivid apple-green; but after six or eight years it may be 60 cm. high or more, depending on conditions. *Picea mariana* 'Nana' is another very beautiful one, making a low, semi-prostrate dome. The short, close-packed needles have a most unusual bluish tinge, particularly in spring. A young plant I put in a large trough where it had more than 30 cm. of soil to grow in, attained a spread of nearly 60 cm. in about seven years and had to be removed to save the neighbours it was swamping. It survived the move in spite of the loss of half its roots and all the soil falling away from those that remained. Now, ten years later, it is a fine specimen spreading out over the stones of a paved area. *Picea abies* 'Nidiformis' with me has grown rather less vigorously, mainly perhaps because it is in a smaller trough (approximately 60 cm. x 30 cm. x 18 cm. deep) where root-run and nourishment are restricted. It was planted in a corner and after about eighteen years is only 50 cm. across and no more than 20 cm. high. Two-thirds of its bulk spills over the side of the trough. Whether you think this is an unfair proportion of space for one plant to occupy is a matter of personal decision. I have allowed it to remain because it still looks healthy and pleases me with its dense, pendent-tipped branches of medium green during the year and its brilliance in spring. *Picea abies* 'Gregoriana' and *P.a.* 'Clanbrassiliana' both form dense balls of extremely close-packed leaves and will take a good deal longer to outgrow their allotted space.

## Shrubs

As well as the conifers, there are a number of other shrubs which are sufficiently dwarf and slow-growing for troughs. *Rhodothamnus chamaecistus* is one, a completely captivating plant when happy, though not always easy to please or even to acquire. It is one of the very few ericaceous plants which is absolutely and reliably lime-tolerant. Very slowly it builds itself up into a twiggy, 15 cm. bushlet, clothed in small, oval, evergreen leaves and in May has exquisite blooms of soft pink filled with striking prominent anthers. *Thymus membranaceus* makes a low grey bush with intensely fragrant leaves and bears white flowers which emerge from curious heads of inflated pink-flushed, apple-green bracts. Its hardiness is slightly suspect in a really fierce winter, especially if it is a few years old. *Helichrysum coralloides* was at first thought to be of doubtful hardiness but has since proved absolutely trustworthy, no matter what winter conditions it is asked to put up with. It is very slow-growing, my oldest plant, now about ten years old, being little over 30 cm. across and about 22 cm. high. As new growth appears in spring the small, close-set, scale-like leaves are densely clothed in white wool but as they age they fold themselves flat against the stems so that only the glossy deep green underside of the leaf is visible with a small line of whiteness round the edges. The effect is to make each stem look like a whipcord with a fascinating snake-skin pattern.

In a large trough some of the really dwarf willows can be tried; planted near the edge, they will have to be prevented from invading the body of the trough but will gradually trail down the sides to good effect. *Salix reticulata* is one of the slowest growers, with beautiful oval, inch-long leaves of polished green, deeply etched with a network of veins. The whole plant rises barely two cm. above ground. *Salix myrsinites* var. *jacquinii* is a little more hasty, with smaller, paler leaves on wiry red-brown stems; in *Salix retusa* the leaves are a pleasant greyish, olive green. All three have little upright catkins in spring, lose their leaves for the winter and are crawlers or sprawlers. *Salix boydii* stands upright and after only a few years of very slow growth assumes the look of a gnarled old veteran, almost as interesting in its winter bareness as in its summer mantle of small, rounded grey leaves. Of rather similar gnarled upright habit, and just as slow growing, is *Ilex crenata* 'Mariesii'. A 30 cm. high specimen is a veteran monster and its small, rounded glossy leaves set at right angles to the stem are evergreen. Also evergreen but more spreading in habit is *Jasminum parkeri* from N.W. India. It is hardy in all but the coldest districts and has typical yellow jasmine flowers spasmodically through the summer. It never seems able to produce a really spectacular display all at once, preferring to spread its charm over several months. The flowers are often followed by small and glossy black berries.

In a lime-free trough you might be successful with *Loiseleuria procumbens*. It is not an easy customer to please and seldom achieves in the garden the pure enchantment it has in its native mountains where, having found a foot-hold in some small crevice or at the foot of a large rock, it will gradually cover the vertical rock-face with a network of thread-like stems and tiny bronze leaves and in early summer swathe itself with a mass of very small starry pink flowers. If you are successful, at least you will have the satisfaction of knowing you have achieved what few other gardeners have managed — especially if it flowers.

Whatever skills you lavish on *Hebe buchananii* 'Minor' you are unlikely to get it to flower. It has never shown me a bloom in twenty years. But it is a real charmer nevertheless, desperately slow-growing — and all the better for that when growing in a trough — making a small mound of tiny, tight-packed, glossy evergreen leaves. *Hebe* 'Carl Teschner' is a hybrid of great value and uncertain parentage raised in New Zealand by the enthusiast whose name it bears. Planted on the edge of a trough it will hang over the edge and reward its owner with a fine summer show of 2-3 cm. tapered spires of clear lavender-blue. It seldom grows more than 30 cm. across or 20 cm. high and is a great addition to our rock gardens as well as our troughs. *Pimelea prostrata* is another very dwarf creeping evergreen which will drape itself decoratively over the edge of any trough. The mat of small grey leaves is adorned by little clusters of stemless creamy flowers in early summer and small berries that look for all the world like a scattering of pearls.

*Genista delphinensis* is an endemic of the Pyrenees and is like a miniaturised form of the vigorous growing *G. sagittalis*. It makes a miniature forest of curious winged and jointed stems no more than 5-7 cm. high and has a wealth of golden gorse-like blooms in late spring. *Daphne cneorum* is unsuitable for trough culture on account of its size and widespreading habit of growth but the so called *Daphne cneorum* var. *album* is very different — very slow growing, absolutely prostrate and with small clusters of creamy-white deliciously scented flowers. I refuse to believe that it is a white-flowered form of what we grow as *D. cneorum*; its true origins and nomenclature have still to be settled. Unfortunately it is a very rare plant. *Petrophytum hendersonii* forms a neat dense dome of pleasant slightly hairy greyish-green leaves and is adorned in early summer with little rounded heads of fluffy, creamy flowers on 5 cm. stems. It scores by being unlike any other plant, but may need some protection from winter wet.

## Plants in Tufa

If you are lucky enough to have got hold of some tufa for your trough, there are a number of plants which will be happier growing in it than anywhere else; an even larger number will grow just as well there as in more conventional places. This means, of course, that you can expand the number of plants you are able to grow in the relatively small area of a trough garden.

Tufa is a variable stone; some of it when newly quarried is extremely soft and crumbly, other types may be reasonably hard, and occasionally it is really solid and rock-like on the outside, though it will be softer and porous inside. If you have any choice, select a medium grade. You will need to make small holes to start your plants in. They should be about 2.5 cm. wide and at least 5—7.5 cm deep. On a vertical or angled face it is best to slant them downwards at an angle of about 45° into the stone, but on or near the top they can be made directly and perpendicularly downwards. With the very soft type of tufa you can often make these holes with an old blunt chisel or gouge, turning it round as it moves in and flicking out the debris every now and then with some tool of slightly smaller bore. If the rock is of the harder type, however, you will have to use a brace fitted with an 2.5 cm. (one inch) bit for which you no longer have much respect. It is wise to make the holes before you do the main planting; you can then afford to swill out the holes with water from a rose-less can to remove any fragments, without also swilling out nearby plants.

It is no good trying to cram full-grown plants into these small holes; much better to grow your own youngsters or choose young, just-established plants from a nurseryman. First shake all the soil from the roots of the young plant, and this is obviously done most easily if the soil is fairly dry. Put just a pinch of nice gritty potting soil into the bottom of the hole with a pencil or something similar. Spread the roots out as much as possible in such a confined space and trickle in more dry soil round the roots, firming as you go with the blunt end of the pencil. If it is possible to encase the roots neatly in the centre of a core of soil, so much the better, but this is often not easy to do and they will end up pressed against one side of the hole with soil filling the remaining space. They usually survive. Take care that the neck of the plant is far enough into the hole to ensure that the plant is not in effect carried aloft on a small trunk of root, like a miniature standard tree; this would mean dangerous and uncomfortable movement in wind. It is a good plan to leave the hole not quite filled with soil and then to press in one or two quite small pieces of rock or chips bringing their tops level with the rock's surface. This will prevent soil being washed out during watering.

Nearly all the Kabschia saxifrages are suitable for such treatment, but they are best placed on the shadier north or east faces of the tufa. On the sunnier slopes they often tend to burn when the full force of the sun strikes them, and you are then left with disfiguring brown patches. *Saxifraga diapensioides* is perfect in such a position, very slowly forming a dense, hard cushion of close-packed, silvery rosettes. It is usually the last of the section to flower, expanding its snowy-white blooms on 2.5cm. stems at the end of March and well into April. *S. tombeanensis* is another species of slow, compact growth, not quite so silvery of leaf but full of character, the flowers of equal whiteness appearing a week or two sooner. *S. caesia*, its smaller relative *S. squarrosa*, and their natural hybrid *S.* x *tyrolensis* are also good; so too is *S. burseriana* with larger flowers on handsome crimson stems and with much more spiny foliage. These are all white, which, come to think of it, is the dominant colour in the wild species of this section of the family. *S. aretioides* is largely responsible for the yellow that appears in so many of the hybrids. It is a nice enough plant in its own right, with tight-packed leaves and two or three rather small flowers of a curious, slightly green-washed yellow to each stem. *S.*

*burseriana* var. *sulphurea* and *S. burseriana* 'Major Lutea', though both pure burserianas as far as looks go, probably have aretioides blood in their veins to give them their sulphur-yellow flowers; both are excellent plants, slow growing and dependable, 'Major Lutea' being the freer flowerer with me. One or two of the other yellows such as *S.* 'Elizabethae', *S.* x apiculata and *S.* 'Haagii' grow very much more vigorously and are best kept out of tufa holes and even out of troughs generally, fine plants though they are in the rock garden. More suitable, if you are still searching for this colour, are *S.* 'Boydii' (the first of the yellow hybrids and still a good plant) and best of all *S.* 'Faldonside' with beautifully rounded blooms of deep colour on 2.5cm., reddish stems.

Among those saxifrages with pink flowers *S.* 'Jenkinsiae' is quite outstanding; vigorous, though not rampant, utterly dependable and producing its enchanting shell-pink flowers with almost unbelievable freedom. *S.* 'Cranbourne' is another very good variety with deep pink flowers freely borne on shorter stems. There are many intermediate colours to choose from; *S.* 'Riverslea' with deep plum-red flowers; *S.* 'Valerie Keevil' of rather similar habit with smallish bright cherry-red blooms; *S.* 'Iris Prichard' with longer stemmed blooms of an unusual and rather beautiful creamy-apricot colour. The choice is almost limitless. If you want really early flowers, *S.* 'Marie Luisa' often shows the white of its petals soon after Christmas; so does *S.* 'Kellereri' though the flowers are small and not of a very good pink. It has the advantage, however, of throwing out blooms at almost any time of the year. These are only a very few members of one section of the vast saxifrage household; there are many others to choose from and nearly all are worth growing. There are few really dowdy Kabschias, hybrid or species.

The next most important section of the saxifrages is known as Euaizoonia. What a name, but what a gift to the Scrabble addict overloaded with vowels! Eight vowels and two consonants must be unique. 'Silver Saxifrage' is a much more pronounceable term and more descriptive, for they nearly all have attractive silvery foliage. Not all are suitable for troughs and very few for growing in tufa, though those which are adaptable to this spartan life are quite excellent. First and foremost *S. cochlearis* 'Minor', which will form a densely-rounded hummock of glowing silver rosettes, each less than a 6 mm. across, has 15 cm. crimson-stemmed spikes bearing sprays of white flowers in late May and June. It is immensely long-lived and almost indestructible. I have a plant I put in a piece of tufa in a stone sink over sixty years ago; it is still there to this day, a solid carapace of silver 30 cm. across, throwing out its quota of snowy blooms with unabated zeal each year. *S. paniculata* (= *aizoon*) var. *baldensis* (more correctly and appropriately it should nowadays be called *S. paniculata* 'Minutifolia') is the only other really suitable 'Silver' for growing in tufa. It forms flatter domes than the last, is not quite so silvery and the flowers are creamy-white.

Various other miscellaneous saxifrages enjoy life in tufa, particularly *S. grisebachii* 'Wisley Variety' from whose wonderfully symmetrical silver rosettes emerge, very early in the year, the most curious and beautiful stems, looking like some nightmare caterpillar clothed in crimson velvet. The actual flowers are tucked away in the tips of these leafy, brilliantly-coloured stems which hold their attraction well on into summer as their length gradually increases. A young plant of *S. retusa* will quickly root right down into tufa as it slowly creeps over its surface, forming a moss-like carpet, only millimetres high, of tiny dark green leaves. The branched, 2.5 cm. high stems each carry several small wine-red blooms in late spring.

In its wild state *Vitaliana primuliflora* (= *Douglasia vitaliana*) usually chooses to grow high in the alps in stony places such as sloping screes or bare roadside banks. In captivity it enjoys life in tufa and flowers freely, particularly in its subspecies *praetutiana*. Collected forms are often much less free with their stemless golden flowers and the loose mats of short-leaved rosettes are not so well silvered. *Draba bryoides* var. *imbricata* makes wonderfully tight, slow-growing packs of tiny, tiny leaves, brown for the winter, changing to vivid emerald with astonishing speed as spring approaches; three or four small, bright golden flowers are carried on each thread-like stem. *Draba aizoides*, with larger, bristly, loose-growing rosettes is good too, flowering very early in the year and often self-sowing in an accommodating, non-invasive way. These are all relatively easy plants to grow, but others such as *Physoplexis comosa, Asperula suberosa, Potentilla nitida* and *Campanula zoysii* are usually much more difficult to please without an alpine house. Yet all four have flourished and flowered with me for a number of years in tufa, and with no nonsense like panes of glass over their heads in winter. I enjoy an alpine house, and believe it to be a necessity, but I also love the great outdoors and expect my plants to do the same; I have no use for disfiguring half-way greenhouses littered about the garden.

Other plants to try in tufa holes are *Myosotis rupicola*, which lives longer and remains dwarfer than it will on a richer diet: many of the smaller androsaces such as *AA. villosa* & var. *jacquemontii*,

*Potentilla nitida* (p. 26 )　　　　　　　　　　　　Photo: AGS Library

*Campanula zoysii* (p. 26)　　　　　　　　　　　　Photo: Mike Ireland

*Androsace villosa* var. *jacquemontii*  (p. 26 )     Photo: AGS Library

*Oxalis enneaphylla* forma (p. 31 )     Photo: Mike Ireland

and *sempervivoides* which usually manage to penetrate all but the hardest-surface tufa with the roots which emerge from their strawberry-like runners; even some of the rarer and more difficult Aretian androsaces such as *AA. pyrenaica, cylindrica* or *vandellii* (= *imbricata*) are worth a trial. *Dianthus musalae\*, D. freynii* and *D. microlepis* all form tight cushions of close-packed leaves and should be happy and free-flowering. The wisdom of planting *Erinus alpinus*, or its several colour forms, in tufa is debatable. It looks right and is a charming plant but, like the rabbit, its private life is a disgrace. It seeds itself so freely and enjoys life so much in tufa that it can easily become a pest. If you are prepared to spend some time removing seedlings which have put themselves in the wrong place, by all means try it. But be warned! *Campanula arvatica* and its beautiful white form, var. *alba*, are about the only campanulas that are completely suitable, though some of the other smaller-growing ones are worth a trial. The real answer to growing plants in tufa is to go on the old maxim of try anything once. The most surprising things happen; I had a plant of the reputedly lime-hating *Lewisia tweedyi* growing and flowering for several years; I have even seen *Calceolaria darwinii*, of all unlikely plants, apparently content with life under such conditions.

*\*D. musalae* does not appear to be a valid name for the dianthus found on Mt. Musala, which authorities regard as synonymous with, or a variety of, *D. microlepis*.

## Plants for Crevices

The plants which will like growing in the crevices between the rocks in your trough are really an extension of those we have just been discussing. If you have not been able to get hold of any tufa, most of the plants you would have grown in tufa will grow between other rocks. All the Kabschia saxifrages are happy when sandwiched in 2—3cm.wide crevices and a much larger number of the 'Silvers' will be suitable. *Saxifraga cochlearis* 'Major' makes firm domes of silvered, 12 mm. rosettes and has pure white flowers; *S.* x *burnatii* has looser rosettes of longer leaves and is equally silver, with many-flowered sprays of white blooms on distinctly arching stems, which make it ideal for a vertical crevice. It is extremely tough and long-lived. *S.* 'Whitehill' has an interesting misty-grey look to its close-packed rosettes and has creamy-white flowers. White, or near-white, is the dominant colour amongst the 'Silvers', but for a minor change *S. paniculata* var. *rosea* comes out pinkish but soon fades, whilst *S.* 'Kathleen Pinsent' is a good clear pink on opening but seems unable to hold its colour for long. *S. cotyledon*, with its forms and hybrids, is usually too vigorous and smothering in troughs; so, too, are the larger members of the race derived from *S. lingulata*, now correctly known as *S. callosa*. Choose your 'Silvers' with care, but one or two should be in every trough, as in every rock garden, for the year-round beauty of their silver leaves. If you have been able to contrive a north-facing crevice, this will be the place to put *Ramonda myconi*; it hates sun and it also hates drought, though it has an astonishing power to revive after a thirsty period. It is unlike any other plant with its flat rosettes of bristly, crinkled, spoon-shaped leaves and short stems bearing three or four flat, mauve, orange-beaked flowers. A north-facing crevice will also accommodate some of the primulas such as *P. marginata* with soft lavender blooms and beautifully powdered, deckle-edged leaves, *P. hirsuta* (= *rubra*) with fine pink flowers on nice short stems and the even brighter *P.* x *berninae* 'Windrush'. Most of the so-called 'pubescens' hybrids prefer some shelter from the full strength of the sun. So too, in my experience, do those lewisias which shelter under the general heading of *L. cotyledon*. This always surprises me slightly; with their thick fleshy leaves one would suspect them of liking an arid, sun-baked position. But when I have tried them outdoors they have always done best in a north-facing position, in as vertical a crevice as possible, where winter damp will be shed from the vulnerable collars of their carrot-like roots. *L.* 'Trevosia' has now lasted ten years and has produced flowers most years.

## Plants for the Flatter Areas

Let us start off here with the most perfect of all alpines, *Gentiana verna*. There is no blue quite so true, and to me it is the distilled essence of every holiday I have spent in the Alps. It is not the difficult plant it is sometimes said to be, but it is not long-lived. In cultivation, two or three years of full and effective life are about as much as one can expect of it. Give it full sun in a soil that will not dry out in summer and has more nourishment in it than most alpines normally need. An excellent companion for it is *Primula farinosa* with little heads of lavender-pink blooms carried at the same modest height, opening at the same time and enjoying the same conditions. One has to be careful with the dianthus family; many are far too vigorous for a small space. *Dianthus alpinus*, meaning the true plant, not the Allwoodii Hybrids which have this name wrongly attached to them, is ideal, making a close clump of short, glossy leaves hidden under glowing pink, speckle-centred flowers on 5 cm. stems; so too is *D. pavonius* (= *neglectus*), so often quoted as being a lime-hater, but happy and permanent in my oolitic limestone and never shy with its flowers. All the small ones mentioned as suitable for growing in tufa will be just as happy on the gritty plains of your trough. Campanulas must be chosen with equal care; some are obviously so sprawling and spreading that they do not need mentioning, but you may be tempted by a nursery potful of *C. cochlearifolia* (= *pusilla*) which is perfect for height but can sometimes run with such zest on its little thread-like roots that it will be all over the trough in no time. An invader of such charm may be acceptable; it is a mixer rather than a throttler; it rather depends on its neighbours.

*Potentilla tabernaemontani* 'Nana' makes neat little tufts of five-part leaves and throws out its small, bright-gold flowers for long periods in summer; a nice companion for it is our native Milkwort, *Polygala calcarea*, with small, oval, glossy leaves and 2.5cm. high heads of inky-blue flowers. It is one of that very small band of completely non-alpine plants which look perfectly right in the most esoteric alpine company. It grows wild only a few miles from here, where it has to straggle and struggle for life amongst grasses; yet in the garden it forms a neat dome of leaves and even in flower rises to barely 5 cm. *Oxalis enneaphylla* is a delectable dwarf, with curious greyish, crimped leaves amongst which the pink or white funnel-shaped flowers nestle in late spring. *Soldanella alpina* can be tried; it tends to be shy-flowering though I suspect that marauding slugs are often the cause of this; its deeply fringed lavender bells are pure enchantment. *Edraianthus pumilio* almost matches it in colour but not in form; its silvery, 2.5cm. long, needle-thin leaves hem in the stemless flowers and it will often self-sow under the right conditions. So will *Gentiana saxosa*, a New Zealander which, like so many plants from that land, has white flowers. It is untypical of the genus, too, in its bronzy, almost strap-shaped leaves. *Saxifraga oppositifolia* has many colour forms, all of which are suitable for the open plains of a trough. They spread very slowly with flat, close-packed clumps of leaves a bare 12mm. high and, sparrows permitting, produce their stemless blooms of crimson, pink, rose or white with unfailing regularity in the very early part of the year.

There are several plants which could almost be classified as miniature ground-cover plants and are suitable for the area we are dealing with. *Antennaria dioica* 'Minima' makes a small ground-hugging carpet of tiny silver-backed leaves and carries its little heads of pink flowers on 2.5 cm. stems and *Thymus serpyllum* 'Minus' forms a very restricted carpet of minute aromatic leaves smothered in early summer with small pink flowerheads. There are other forms of both *Antennaria dioica* and *Thymus serpyllum*, but all of them are far too lusty for troughs. *Arenaria purpurascens* hides its flat carpet of small glistening leaves under a mass of starry flowers in spring. My father and I found a fine deep-coloured form of this in the Cantabrian Mountains and called it *A.p.* 'Elliott's Variety'.

## Trailers

Two or three carefully chosen plants put at the edge of a trough so that they can grow over and down the sides can add greatly to the general effect. Sometimes they may need restraining either by bending in the right direction or by complete removal of small pieces, but few will resent such persuasion. *Dryas octopetala* 'Minor' is one of the best of all, a perfect half-size version of its bigger, better-known parent, the Mountain Avens. The small, creamy, golden-centred flowers are followed by fascinating silky seed-heads. *Helianthemum oelandicum* (= *alpestre*) has many good forms, some with small greyish leaves clothing a network of prostrate stems, gay with golden flowers in early summer. Even better perhaps, particularly if space is restricted, is *Helianthemum* 'oblongatum' without ever having found any valid authority for such a name. It is smaller than the last with tiny, oval, polished leaves on crimson stems and the same golden flowers. *Linum suffruticosum* subsp.*salsoloides* 'Nanum' clothes its creeping stems in myriads of very short, needle-like leaves and has charming, just-off-white, funnel flowers on 5—7cm. high stems. Phloxes need choosing carefully; most forms of *P. subulata* are much too vigorous but several forms of *P. douglasii* keep well to heel, specially *P.d.* 'Violet Queen' which will smother itself in its rounded blooms of uniform colour.

All the trailers mentioned so far are evergreen, or nearly so, and it is worth keeping in mind when selecting trough plants generally that the more evergreen plants you have, the greater will be the interest in winter. Two plants that always look happy when spilling over the edge of a trough but which retire below ground for the winter are *Sedum cauticola*, with trailing stems of fleshy, dove-grey leaves and flat heads of crimson flowers in September and October, and *Cyananthus microphyllus*, each of whose hanging stems terminates in a beautiful bloom of amethyst-blue, at the same time of year.

## Finishing Touches

When the building and planting of your trough is finished, the final act should be to cover all bare soil with stone chippings or pea gravel. There are several good reasons for this. If what I have written so far has had any impact, you will have filled your trough largely with dwarfish plants sheltering under the general heading of alpines, however widely you interpret that word. Most of these will have been used to growing in the wild in rather stony soil and somehow have a naked look against the bare soil; so the chips will give a more natural appearance. A planted trough without chippings always looks to me like a man who has put on his shirt and suit but forgotten his tie. But there are also more practical reasons; a covering of chippings helps to conserve moisture to a certain extent by slowing down evaporation; it will lessen any caking of the soil surface and, since most of the flowers when they appear will be only 2.5—5cm. from the ground, the chippings will prevent heavy rain splashing soil on to them and spoiling their beauty. 6—9mm. chippings are suitable, or alternatively washed pea gravel. They do not need to be spread more than 12mm. thick. Tuck them carefully under the cushion plants so that the vulnerable necks of these plants are free of standing moisture.

## Maintenance

People often ask me how often I replant my troughs. My answer is always the same. Never, not completely, anyway! Plants die, of course, or they may take up more space than their beauty or interest warrants; sometimes one even gets tired of them. When any of these things happen the offending plant is removed. Then by scraping out as much of the old soil as possible, with minimum disturbance to neighbours' roots, fresh soil can be put in and the area replanted. The remaining plants are left established and undisturbed. Apart from this sort of activity, very little maintenance is needed. Watering has to be done of course, but this is less than would have to be done with, say, chrysanthemums in pots. The thick stone sides of a trough are much better insulators than pots of either clay or plastic, so drying out is not so rapid. The aim should be never to allow the soil to become bone dry during spells of hot weather; on the other hand, overwatering can be fatal. It is an often-quoted but very true axiom that more alpines are killed by over-watering than by under-watering. The great majority have an in-built survival kit enabling them to cope with near-drought conditions for quite long periods, but few of them can cope with a permanent bog. You soon learn to know by hunch when water is needed, but if in doubt all you need do is to scratch away the surface chippings and see how things are getting on. When water is given it should be given plentifully; with a deep trough, till it is running over the sides and then, after a ten minute wait, the same again, by which time the water should be running out of the drainage hole. If the soil and drainage are right, you will not be creating the much-feared bog, and no more should be needed for a day or two, even in the hottest weather. Remember, though, that a kitchen sink, with only 5—7.5cm. of soil depth, will dry out very much more quickly than an old pump trough with a foot or more of soil.

A little gentle feeding is called for occasionally, but provided the plants flower reasonably well and look healthy, one does not want the plants to grow too fast, so feeding should be minimal. I usually give all my troughs a dressing of Hoof and Horn about the first week of March, at the rate of about a handful to each square metre of surface area. Bone Meal would no doubt do nearly as well, though it is a little slower to release its nourishment and, on analysis, not quite so complete a plant food. Both are relatively slow-acting and long-lasting, so if your enthusiasm gets a bit out of hand with these materials, no great harm will be done by either. I would never use a general garden fertiliser on my troughs; such sudden boost could be catastrophic; but friends who have needed to give their plants a slightly faster encouragement than Hoof and Horn would give, have used some of the bottled liquid fertilisers such as Bio or Phostrogen, in a weak solution, without any ill effects.

## Conclusion

In putting together these thoughts on trough gardening I have taken it for granted that the main objective in planting a trough with alpines is to create a rock garden in miniature and to grow as many plants as possible in the relatively confined space available. I am convinced that this is the most satisfying way of going about things. But it is not the only way. Troughs can be put to many other useful and practical purposes. In a limy district for instance, they can hold an isolated pocket of lime-free soil to enable you to grow the lime-haters; in an over-sunny garden they can be put on the north side of the house to provide shade for those plants which need it. In a small quern or mortar you can grow a single specimen of one plant or in something rather larger you may prefer to have several different members of the same genus, sempervivums for instance, or the Silver or Kabschia saxifrages. I have seen superb specimens of quite large troughs or sinks planted with a dozen or more different kinds of Sempervivum which give a wonderfully varied year-round interest. Another fine trough I know, more than 1.5m. long, is planted as a miniature Pinetum with a collection of really slow-growing dwarf conifers.

On my nursery I always had three or four troughs each containing two or three dozen *Gentiana verna* and nothing else. For the whole of May they are a wonderful sight — solid sheets of that vivid, deep, true blue which is unique in the plant world. They caused much comment and, I suspect, not a little envy. The trouble is, of course, that for the remaining eleven months of the year they are relatively uninteresting. My only motive for such imbalance was the seed they produce from which came the many thousands of this plant I produced and sold each year.

The thirty or more troughs I have about the place fulfil all these purposes and several more besides (I even allow my wife to grow petunias in one!) and I get pleasure from them all. They vary in size from a Yorkshire quern (grinding mill) holding no more than a couple of handfuls of soil to a Saxon stone coffin weighing nearly a ton. This took a trailer and tractor, six men and several gallons of beer to get into position but it fits me like a glove. I tested it for size before planting began.

# Index to Plants in the Text